OUR TEMPLE

WEDDING
Planner

OUR TEMPLE

SUSAN EVANS McCLOUD

EAGLE
GATE

SALT LAKE CITY, UTAH

Library of Congress Cataloging-in-Publication Data

McCloud, Susan Evans.
    Our temple wedding planner / Susan Evans McCloud.
        p.   cm.
    ISBN 1-57008-796-2 (pbk.)
    1. Marriage—Religious aspects—Church of Jesus Christ of Latter-day Saints.   2. Wedding etiquette.   I. Title

BX8641 .M23 2002
395.2'2'088283—dc21   2001006715

Printed in the United States of America   21239-6933
Edwards Brothers Incorporated, Ann Arbor, MI

10   9   8   7   6   5   4   3   2   1

This book is dedicated to my daughters,
Heather, Jennie, Rebeccah, Morag, Mairi, and Emily;
and to my granddaughters, Afton and Katie Jean

CONTENTS

PREFACE

There is no love like yours. There will be no other life, no history like yours. Because you are uniquely you, this wedding should be the celebration of a lifetime—your lifetime: the bright, singing focal point of your dreams, your hopes, your beauty, your womanhood.

In the midst of all the work, organization, frustration, and change, remember the ideal. Hold it close to you. Use it to warm you, calm you, cheer you, and fan your loveliness into full bloom.

Throughout your mortal life, throughout your eternal life, this day will remain precious and sacred. But the practicalities must, too, be dealt with. Having married off three daughters and one son, having watched and listened to the concerns of girls during and following their marriage days, I submit the following pages in hopes that they will help you to plan and select, organize and achieve, a marriage experience which will suit your needs and realities—and match your expectations.

But through it all, remember—you are the bride! Nothing can take the glory of that moment away from you.

—Susan Evans McCloud

INTRODUCTION

The most important thing to remember on your wedding day is the eternal significance of the temple marriage ceremony. This is the ceremony that brings you together with the approval of Heavenly Father and seals you to each other for time and all eternity. This sacred covenant is one of the most vital gospel covenants you will ever make and is an essential part of your eternal salvation. Do not let any other celebrations overshadow this monumental event. Parties, dresses, flowers, cakes, and presents are all secondary and pale in comparison to your actual temple marriage. As you plan your wedding and inevitably get caught up in the details, remember that your *wedding day* is only the beginning; your *marriage* is eternal and requires preparation on a spiritual level.

This book will help you plan the events surrounding the celebration of your marriage. It gives guidelines for a typical LDS wedding for a young couple. Remember that there are many options to consider in addition to the traditional setting outlined here. For example, many couples do not want to have a wedding reception. Instead they may have a family dinner at a favorite restaurant the night before the wedding. Or they may use the money they would have spent on a wedding reception to pay for their honeymoon. Other couples have their reception the night before, instead of on the wedding day. Some couples like their reception to be a more casual affair; a barbecue where everyone is wearing jeans and enjoying a cookout is another way to celebrate a wedding.

Many couples who do have wedding receptions have much less involved ones than what is outlined in this book. Their wedding party consists of only the bride and groom and their parents—no bridesmaids, maids of honor, groomsmen, or flower girls. When divorces, deaths, and remarriages complicate the issue of which parents to include in a wedding line, some bridal couples may forfeit the idea of a line altogether, or have a simple line consisting of just the bride and groom.

Couples for whom this is a second marriage will likely not have a reception and may not want pictures on the temple grounds. They most likely will choose a more intimate way to celebrate their wedding with only family and close friends.

Some couples don't have a wedding breakfast or luncheon the day of the wedding. Others have a late afternoon wedding with a family dinner afterward or the night before.

There is no one correct way to celebrate your wedding. Plan what you want and what works best for you and your circumstances. The information in this book should be used and adapted in a manner that best helps you. These suggestions are not meant to be taken as a list of hard-and-fast rules. Accept the material that helps you and use it; feel free to disregard the rest. The purpose of this book is only to aid, assist, and enhance.

1

FIRST THINGS FIRST

You are getting married! This is the celebration of a lifetime. In the months and weeks before your wedding there will be so much to do, so many emotions, and so many people involved. At times it may be hard to keep your focus. But things will go more smoothly if you remember your priorities. Your major considerations for this wedding should be:

1. *The marriage ceremony.* You are taking the most important step of your mortal and eternal life. Try to focus your senses and appreciation on the marriage ceremony itself. Give yourself time to ponder and prepare, to understand and be ready.

2. *Time.* Set a date that is realistic (even if you are getting married in a between-school break). Make sure the date selected is something your parents can live with, as well as yourselves. And take into special consideration time for travel, particularly if there is not a temple nearby, or if either set of parents does not live close.

3. *Money.* Plan together a workable budget that will fit within your means. Typically, these costs are shared by the bride and groom and their two families. Any agreed upon assignment of responsibility between families is acceptable, but it is important to discuss expectations and financial realities in advance.

- Start Early. Whether you have six months or six weeks, they will quickly slip through your fingers. Organize as much as you can as soon as possible.
- Be Practical. Ask yourself, Will it work in terms of our resources and circumstances? Is it worth the cost and effort?
- List Priorities. Ask yourself such questions as: Do we want a longer honeymoon or a more expensive ring? Do I want an elaborate dress or more money to spend on the pictures? Do we want a big reception with light refreshments or a smaller gathering with a sit-down meal?
- Remember the people you love. You need them now as much or more than ever.

If there is anything better than to be loved, it is loving.
—Anonymous

2

GETTING STARTED

As you begin your engagement, there are several important things you will want to address first. These include the engagement ring, meeting each other's parents if you haven't already, officially announcing your engagement, setting your wedding date, creating a budget, and structuring a calendar of events.

THE RING

Perhaps even before the engagement comes the matter of the ring. Remember that this is a big financial and emotional investment. Whether you pick it out together or he surprises you, you will want to:

- Shop around and compare.
- Consider only reputable jewelry merchants and obtain a written guarantee of the stone's value.
- Be honest about your price range and stick within it.
- If you finance the purchase, check for the lowest interest rates and shortest possible borrowing terms.
- Consider the selection of an antique ring. These are often less costly and come with unusual choices of stones and settings, as well as an aura and a history of their own.
- Ask about proper care for your particular stone and setting.

Meeting the Parents

You would not be here, enjoying this day and looking forward to all the wonderful days ahead, if it had not been for the people who wanted you and brought you into the world. These special people should be treated with affection and care. Involve the parents of both the bride and the groom and be sensitive to such issues as divorce, remarriages, stepparents, or the death of a parent. As soon as possible, arrange a meeting that will not threaten or inconvenience any of the parties. Perhaps several meetings among various parents is warranted, determined by time, place, and circumstances. Try to accommodate your parents' needs, and support any plans and preparations they may want to make. In other words, involve them.

Tips

Fathers may have varying degrees of interest and availability, but make certain both mothers are invited to participate in the wedding planning. Ask them to comment on plans and decisions, and to offer their help and opinions. You do not have to act on these suggestions, but it is both thoughtful and respectful to listen and let them be part of the fun.

Remember that even if you do not know or feel comfortable around your future mother-in-law right now, this woman is the woman who loved and prayed for your fiancé and helped him to become who he is. Your relationship with your mother-in-law could, and should, be one of the most intimate, caring, and rewarding relationships of your life.

Official Announcement

We're getting married! After spreading the glad tidings by word of mouth, you may want a more formal announcement. The announcement could be in a local newspaper, your ward bulletin, or a family newsletter.

Make sure to include in the announcement:
- your names in full, and your parents' names
- schooling and present job positions
- missionary experience or military record, if any
- interesting awards, achievements, or positions
- expected wedding date (or season of the year if the date hasn't been determined)
- photo, black and white glossy (if desired)

Tips

Check newspaper rates and policies before submitting your announcement. Many newspapers charge by the number of lines used.

Including a photograph may be an additional cost. Find out beforehand if the photograph will be returned.

Make sure information is sent to cities where your parents live, if different from your own.

SETTING THE DATE

Ideally, you should allow at least six months to plan your wedding, but it can be done in a shorter length of time if you are flexible. Many LDS couples choose to have much shorter engagements. A vital part of this key decision is selecting and scheduling the temple (see chapter 3). Traditionally, the most popular months to wed are June, August, September, and December. If you are considering a wedding during those months, you will need to schedule the temple and reserve a reception site further in advance. Take your time with this decision. Make sure your choice is convenient, workable, and as close to "just right" as possible.

Tips

Consider your budget (see chapter 4) in selecting the time and place for your wedding. If an at-home reception best fits your budget, time of year and weather considerations may be a larger factor in determining the date.

If the budget is tight, consider a Tuesday, Wednesday, or Thursday, when reception centers may offer lower rates.

Remember that most temples are closed on Mondays and major holidays.

Verify that a sealing room is available at the temple of your choice before finalizing the wedding date and booking a reception site.

BEGIN YOUR BUDGET

Sit down together and map out:
- your needs
- your priorities
- your desires
- your resources

Do not forget to budget past the date of the wedding for:
- honeymoon expenses
- new home costs such as moving expenses, utilities set up, deposits/rent, phone hookup, furniture and household needs, and food and kitchen supplies

See chapter 4 for detailed information for planning your budget.

CREATE A CALENDAR

Begin now to set deadlines for making wedding preparations. Using the Wedding Checklist at the end of this book as a guide, schedule all important activities and deadlines on your calendar as soon as possible.

3
THE TEMPLE

The purpose and the heart of your wedding day is the temple sealing ceremony that will unite the bride and groom for all eternity. Do not overshadow this all-important ordinance with the trappings of celebration. The sacred sealing of husband and wife is an act of worship, a gift from your Heavenly Father, a perfect moment when earth and heaven are combined in order to bless you. Savor it. Honor it. Let the sweet spirit of that ceremony go with you throughout all the hours of your wedding day.

THE ENDOWMENT

The endowment ordinance is a different and separate ceremony from the sealing ceremony. The bridal couple must have received their individual endowments before they can be sealed together as husband and wife.

If you have not been endowed in the temple earlier, you may want to plan your endowment session at least a week, or perhaps even a month, prior to your wedding date. Many brides find that they are more focused and better able to comprehend and enjoy their first temple experience if it is somewhat in advance of their wedding day. However, circumstances sometimes require that the couple receive their endowments and be sealed in marriage on the same day. Whatever you decide, your primary goal should be to learn and appreciate what is being offered to you in the house of the Lord.

Temples have special sessions for first-time endowments, called "live" endowment sessions. Be sure to check the temple schedule for times when these sessions are offered. Temple workers can tell you how far in advance of the session you will need to arrive at the temple, but about one hour early is customary.

Throughout the bride's endowment session, she will be accompanied by an endowed female escort of her choice—usually a mother, mother-in-law, sister, or other special person. That individual will be by her side at all times. If an escort is not available, a temple worker will be happy to provide assistance. Often the groom has already received his endowment before the bride receives hers. Ideally, your fiancé will be with you to share in your first-time temple experience in special ways allowed the two of you only this one time. Other family members and close friends may also want to be involved (see the chapter on charts and worksheets at the end of this book for a worksheet on making a list of guests for the temple marriage ceremony).

You will need to bring a pair of regular temple garments with you to put on as part of the initiatory session. It is advisable to own six to seven pairs of garments so that you have clean underclothing without having to do laundry more than once a week. If you are not certain what styles or materials you will like best, experiment at first with one each of several fabrics and styles until you find one that best suits you.

If your means will allow, it is wonderful to be able to purchase your own temple clothing. That way whenever you attend the temple, you can wear again the sacred clothing in which you were sealed to your husband—the clothing you were wearing when your lives together began. If you cannot afford all the items, choose one or two that you can purchase and keep using through the years ahead. If possible, select a lovely temple gown to wear when you go through to be endowed; it will remind you of that glorious experience every time you wear it. If that is not practical, temples have a selection of bridal dresses appropriate for the live endowment session. Most temples also have temple clothing available to rent. However, be aware that the smaller temples do not have laundry facilities, and regular temple clothing is generally not available to rent at those locations.

Temple Preparation and Interviews

You and your groom will be required to schedule and attend interviews with your bishop and stake president in order to obtain what is called a "live sealing" recommend.

Your bishop should explain some of the procedures for you, and instruct and counsel you concerning marriage and the sacred covenants you will be taking upon yourself. Some bishops request or allow both partners to attend one another's marriage interviews. Whether this occurs or not, you ought to plan some spiritual time with your fiancé. This could include:

- evenings when you discuss your feelings, fears, expectations, and testimonies.
- visits to the temple together.
- scripture reading.
- serious discussion concerning the kind of household you hope to establish, and the things which are most important and sacred to you.

If this first level of a spiritual foundation is in place, you will enter into the marriage with united spirits and with a confidence in one another which will make the experience sweet and more rewarding. Yes, this is a busy, demanding time for you, but what is more important than this preparation for your eternal marriage? Allow time for this spiritual growth in your life and you will be blessed.

Selecting a Temple

Choosing which temple you will be married in is a very personal decision. It is based not only on practicality (which temple is within easiest travel distance), but also on your own spiritual desires and past spiritual experiences.

Do all that you can to invite the Spirit of the Lord to influence your decision. If you have always loved the Manti Temple, but all of your wedding party is centered in Salt Lake or Logan, consider taking out your endowments in Manti with just a few close family members and friends. Or, make a special temple trip to a regular temple session the week, or even the day, before your wedding so that it becomes part of the spiritual experience connected with your sealing and marriage.

Check temple schedules, availability, and procedure for endowment sessions and for sealings. This might influence your final decision to an unexpectedly large degree.

RESERVING A SEALING ROOM

It is important to reserve a sealing room and time for the date you have set. This should be done as soon as possible. During busy months (June, August, September, and December), you may want to have a couple of alternate date possibilities.

You will need to have an idea of the number of people who will attend the wedding ceremony in order to reserve a sealing room. Temples have a few larger capacity sealing rooms, as well as smaller rooms. Generally, sealing rooms do not hold more than fifty people. Rooms directly off the celestial room are used only for sealing ceremonies that directly follow an endowment session. Seating in these rooms is usually limited.

Remember, temple workers will be happy to answer your questions and will send information to help in your preparations. You will need to check with the specific temple for exact information and procedure.

SCHEDULING CONSIDERATIONS

Do you want an early morning sealing? Late morning? Late afternoon, followed by a dinner reception or the reception held the following day? Choose carefully what will be most comfortable and practical for you and your groom, and for the wedding party as a whole, particularly if there are groups or individuals who will be traveling considerable distances.

One of the first decisions you will need to make is whether your wedding day will include a live endowment session, a regular temple session, or the sealing ceremony only. If you plan to take out your endowments on the same day as the sealing ceremony, you will need to allow approximately four hours to complete both ordinances. Be careful of overscheduling your wedding day. Some couples are so overscheduled on their wedding day that they are thoroughly and completely exhausted by the time their wedding night finally arrives.

If you have received your endowment prior to the date of the wedding, the time at the temple will be much shorter on the wedding day. The sealing ceremony itself will take about thirty minutes, but you will need to allow extra time before the ceremony for prewedding instructions and details. A temple worker at the temple you choose can give you a good idea of how much time to allow for this. Typically, the bride and her escort, the groom and his escort (if necessary), and both witnesses will need to be at the temple at least an hour to an hour and a half before the sealing ceremony. That makes an early morning ceremony very early morning indeed! You will also need to reserve time after the sealing ceremony if you want pictures taken on the temple grounds with family members and friends.

Try to avoid scheduling things too closely together. Make sure there is ample time between events so that you do not feel hurried or distracted, especially during this most important part of your wedding day.

The Sealer

Each temple has workers who have been ordained and assigned as sealers. Many sealers will ask the wedding couple questions and give advice in the time before the actual ceremony. During the day or two before the ceremony take a few moments to think about:

- how you met and why you chose one another.
- what special qualities you admire most in each other.
- what it is you desire most in the life you are planning together.

The sealer will give you good advice that he is inspired to receive before he performs the marriage ceremony. Try to pay attention to what he is saying. You may also want your mother or a friend to remind you afterwards of the counsel he gave, so you can write it in your journal. His advice will be good words to live by for you and your new husband.

WITNESSES

The temple will provide you with forms to fill out indicating the names of the men you select to serve as official witnesses to the sealing ceremony. Usually the two fathers, or other worthy family priesthood holders, are asked to fulfill this special role.

RINGS

Following the ceremony, the sealer will provide time for the bridal couple to exchange rings in the sealing room. Or the couple may opt to exchange the rings in private later.

GUESTS

Generally, guests to your temple sealing should be limited to family and very close friends. The seating capacity of the sealing rooms is not large, and only those who are closest to you should be invited to share in this sacred ordinance. Guests should be invited to the sealing ceremony by a separate invitation, which may be in the form of an enclosure card with the reception invitation. (See chapter 9 for more detailed information on creating a guest list for the temple marriage ceremony and chapter 10 on announcements and invitations.) It is essential to find out from the temple what time your wedding party should arrive. You may want to tell your guests to arrive fifteen minutes prior to the specified time because late guests may not be able to attend the wedding ceremony.

As a general guideline, if the sealing ceremony is immediately preceded by a live or regular endowment session, guests will be asked to arrive approximately 30 to 45 minutes before the endowment session and will be dressed in their temple clothes for the wedding ceremony.

Guests attending only the sealing ceremony should not be asked to dress in white, unless the sealing room must be entered from the celestial room. Appropriate chapel dress is required for the sealing ceremony, and women's pants are not allowed. Wedding guests should be in the marriage waiting room at least 30 minutes prior to the ceremony, or as instructed by the specific temple. Guests must bring their current temple recommends with them in order to attend.

Remember that it is customary to include all your wedding guests, not just those in attendance at the temple, in any wedding breakfast or luncheon celebration that directly follows the sealing ceremony.

Be especially thoughtful of family and friends who are not able to enter the temple. Many temples provide lovely places for them to wait during the ceremony, if they would like. Try to project a time for them to arrive which will not require much tedious waiting on their behalf—perhaps at the end of the sealing ceremony when you can come out to greet them and make them feel welcome. This is a natural time, just before the picture-taking begins and the wedding party gathers on the temple grounds to welcome the newly married couple as they leave the temple.

Tip

Appoint an adult who will not be attending the sealing ceremony to bring and take care of children you desire to be part of the family photographs when you come out of the temple.

WEDDING ATTIRE

See chapter 6 for detailed information on temple-ready gowns and appropriate wedding attire for the bride. The groom will wear regular temple ordinance clothes. The parents of the bridal couple should wear "Sunday best" rather than the more formal dresses or tuxedos they might plan to wear for the reception.

You may want to have a bridal bouquet and the mothers' and grandmothers' corsages, along with the groom's and fathers' boutonnieres available for picture-taking on the temple grounds after the sealing ceremony. This can be arranged through your florist or by asking a friend to deliver them for you.

PHOTOGRAPHS

Cameras are not permitted inside the temple, so arrangements should be made to meet the photographer either before or after the ceremony for pictures on the temple grounds. The photographer may wait in the temple foyer/waiting room, or in another location recommended by temple workers, until the appointed time. If the bride plans to wear a temple-owned gown for the sealing ceremony, she may bring her wedding dress and accessories to wear for the photographs. The groom may also wish to bring his tuxedo to wear for photographs. However, bridesmaids and groom's attendants should reserve their wedding attire for the reception.

MISCELLANEOUS GUIDELINES

In keeping with the sacred nature of temples, guests are requested to refrain from acts of celebration that might detract from a spirit of reverence, such as throwing rice or confetti on temple grounds, horn honking, and the use of other noisemakers. Car decorating is also not appropriate near temple grounds.

There is a passion of reverence mingling with the love of an honest man for a pure girl.

—L. Malet

4
MONEY MATTERS

Love is in abundance, but funds are often not. "What matters most?" is a question you and your groom have to keep answering together. Remember: things always cost more than it seems they will. And there will be last-minute and hidden costs to deal with as well. Better to be pleasantly surprised than tense, at your wit's end, and overextended.

Take time to explore options and find bargains. Remember that years from now the cut corners won't be remembered, but the atmosphere, the adventures, the emotions, and the discoveries made in planning your wedding will.

WHO PAYS FOR WHAT?

There are no absolute rules regarding the allocation of wedding expenses, so it is important that both the bride's and groom's families are involved in this decision. The following lists indicate typical costs associated with a wedding and the traditional responsibility for those expenditures.

The bride and her family usually pay for:

- invitations and announcements
- bride's dress, veil, and accessories
- groom's wedding ring

- gift for groom (optional)
- bridesmaids' dresses*
- gifts for bride's attendants
- flowers for bride's attendants
- bridesmaid luncheon (optional)
- own attire and travel costs
- bride's medical exam and blood test
- reception costs**
- photography and videography
- bride's personal trousseau and needs

The groom and his family usually pay for:

- bride's engagement and wedding rings
- marriage license
- own attire and travel costs
- bride's bouquet, mothers' and grandmothers' corsages, and all boutonnieres
- wedding breakfast or luncheon
- gift for bride (optional)
- tuxedo rental for groom and fathers
- tuxedo rental for groom's attendants*
- gifts for groom's attendants
- complete honeymoon trip and expenses

Attendants usually pay for:

- any travel costs
- bridal shower hosted by maid of honor and bridesmaids
- bachelor party hosted by best man and groom's attendants
- a wedding gift

  * *It is acceptable for the bridemaids and groomsmen to pay for their own attire.*

  ** *It is important to note that if more than one reception (or a reception and an open house) is being given, the bride's parents are responsible only for the expenses associated with the reception they host.*

- Talk with your parents, who often pay most of these costs, about the dollar amount they are planning to spend for the wedding. It may be that one family is more able than another to contribute to the wedding expenses.
- Develop a plan well in advance and within the confines of your financial realities.
- Overestimate, rather than underestimate!
- Create a wish list of nonessentials for any leftover funds.

I need your love as a touchstone of my existence. It is the Sun which breathes life into me.

—Juliette Drouet to Victor Hugo

5

THE WEDDING PARTY

Once your priorities and budget have been determined, you should have a good idea of how elaborate or simple a wedding to plan. You will want to keep those considerations in mind in selecting the bride's and groom's attendants.

There are no hard-and-fast rules with regard to the number and size of a wedding party, and the role of the wedding party is certainly different for a temple marriage than for other weddings. Traditionally, the wedding party consists of a maid (or matron) of honor, a best man, bridesmaids (or junior bridesmaids if between the ages of 10 and 16), groom's attendants, and flower girls. The configuration of your wedding party is a personal decision and should be made based on your individual circumstances and desires.

Select members of your wedding party as soon as possible, preferably six months prior to the wedding. To prevent any misunderstandings, it is important to let them know what expenses and time their participation will involve.

HINTS FOR THE BRIDE

- Do not be pressured into a profusion of bridesmaids. It simply may not be possible for you to please everyone. Be kind, but also be wise, realistic, and firm.
- As soon as possible, let your attendants know what you expect

of them and what the schedule and needs of the wedding celebration will be.

- Consider a party to acquaint all of the bride's and groom's attendants with each other as preparations get underway.
- Let your attendants help, especially if they are willing, and delegate certain responsibilities and tasks.
- Involve your attendants in the selection of their dresses (see chapter 8).

MAID OR MATRON OF HONOR

The maid or matron of honor is chosen by the bride. She is often the bride's sister or closest friend, but can be any woman you love and admire. Her responsibilities include:

- Assisting the bride with planning the wedding and managing details, which might include shopping for bridal attire, addressing invitations, and tracking gifts.
- On the wedding day, helping keep the bride on schedule, helping the bride change into going-away clothes after the reception, mailing wedding announcements after the wedding, and returning any rented items, such as the wedding dress or slip.
- Attending all prewedding and wedding celebrations.
- Hosting an engagement or wedding shower for the bride, if desired.

THE BEST MAN

The best man, chosen by the groom, is usually the groom's best friend, brother, or other male relative. Responsibilities of the best man include:

- Assisting the groom with prewedding details. Helping with duties such as: making sure the marriage license and bride's ring are taken to the temple, arranging the bridal couple's departure for their honeymoon, and returning rented tuxedos after the wedding.

- Giving a "toast" to the bride and groom at a wedding breakfast or luncheon, if the bridal couple desires.
- Attending all wedding celebrations.

BRIDESMAIDS

Bridesmaids are chosen by the bride, and are often the bride's friends, sisters, cousins, and sisters of the groom. Responsibilities of the bridesmaids include:
- Assisting with wedding details as requested by the bride.
- Attending prewedding celebrations as requested.
- Attending all wedding day celebrations.

GROOM'S ATTENDANTS

Groom's attendants are chosen by the groom and are often the groom's brothers, cousins, and close friends, or the bride's brothers. Responsibilities of the groom's attendants include:
- Assisting with duties requested by the groom, which may include arranging transportation to the temple, to the wedding breakfast or luncheon, or to the reception for family members of the bridal couple or special out-of-town guests.
- Helping direct guests throughout the reception, if requested.
- Arranging transportation of the wedding gifts from the reception to the home of the bride's parents or other desired location.

FLOWER GIRLS

Flower girls are usually between the ages of four and eight and can be selected from both the bride's and the groom's family. They are not required to attend prewedding celebrations, but are usually in attendance at wedding day celebrations. Traditionally a flower girl carries a basket filled with loose rose petals or flowers that are strewn in the path of the bridal couple.

GIFTS OF APPRECIATION

It is customary for the bride and groom to present small gifts of appreciation to their attendants. You may also wish to acknowledge and honor mothers and fathers, grandmothers, and others who help with the wedding, as the budget allows. The gifts may be presented at a bridesmaids' luncheon or another gathering prior to the wedding. The following suggestions may spark your own ideas and creativity.

Bridal Attendants

- pretty box with a little trinket tucked inside
- piece of jewelry to be worn with their wedding attire and after
- elegant, white handkerchief for the temple (perhaps embroidered with the recipient's initials)
- special hair adornment for the wedding day
- bottle of perfume
- silver or crystal frame to hold a photograph from the wedding
- special book of poetry and an elegant bookmark
- CD of music with special meaning
- engraved pen and/or fancy journal
- nice vase for flowers
- decorative pillow
- note cards or stationery
- candle and candle holder

Groom's Attendants

- cuff links to be worn with wedding attire
- pen and pencil set
- nice manicure kit
- leather wallet
- silver letter opener (perhaps engraved with the recipient's initials)
- picture frame for a wedding photograph
- watch or desk clock

- Use your ingenuity, within the limits of your budget, to present something with special meaning that will be a permanent keepsake of you and your wedding.
- The gifts may be identical for each attendant, or you may opt to buy individual gifts that are similarly priced.
- Purchase gifts as far in advance as possible. Wrap them and tuck them away until you need them. One thing done and accomplished!
- Add a personal note of affection and appreciation. This expression will be cherished long after the gift has been given.

Now she seemed merry as a lark; in her lover's genial presence, she glanced like some soft glad light. How beautiful she grew in her happiness.

—Charlotte Brontë

6

BRIDE'S ATTIRE

Your wedding gown is *the* dress of your life! Make sure the style and fit complement your personality, coloring, height, and body type. Use the following guidelines to help you in this important quest.

FINDING THE PERFECT DRESS

- Some women wish to be married in their mother's dress or a dress that is a family heirloom. If you choose this option, find out about necessary alterations, sizing, and cleaning as early as possible.
- Start early. Stores often carry only sample dresses for you to try on. You may need 3 to 4 months for your gown to be special ordered in the correct color and size. If you are ordering a gown, make sure it will arrive at least six to eight weeks before the wedding to ensure plenty of time for making alterations, selecting accessories, and taking a bridal portrait.
- Go prepared to try on gowns with the underclothes you will wear for the wedding. If you have not yet been to the temple for your endowments, keep in mind the temple garment when trying on dresses. Shoes are usually purchased after the dress, to match.
- Allow plenty of time for shopping, and remember that some stores require appointments to try on gowns. If possible, avoid shopping on Saturday.

- Make sure the dress fits comfortably and is not confining or too tight. If you are between sizes, order the larger size and have it tailored to fit. Remember that it is much easier to make a dress smaller than it is to make it larger. It is not always possible to have a gown enlarged.
- Keep it modest. See the guidelines for temple-ready dresses later in this chapter. But remember, many dresses that have low backs or necklines, or that are sleeveless, can be beautifully altered into modest gowns. Some dresses lend themselves more readily to such alterations than others. Be sure to ask the staff on hand about alterations as you try on dresses.
- Choose what *you* want—not what your mother, sister, or best friend wants.
- Ask around for stores in your area with good reputations. Check the reputation of any store or boutique before making a purchase. If possible, talk to someone who has bought a wedding dress from the same establishment.
- Ask if the store offers a discount for purchasing accessories or attire for other members of the bridal party.
- Some bridal shops will discount a floor model or discontinued styles of dresses. Before you agree to purchase a discounted dress, determine the conditions of the sale and how the discount is applied.
- A deposit of one-third to one-half of the cost is usually required to order a dress. Before you place your order, check the store's exchange and cancellation policies carefully. Get everything in writing, including the delivery date. This may prove important, even if it doesn't seem so at the time. Find out if the store will guarantee the date of delivery.
- Ask for an estimate of alteration fees before ordering a gown. If the store offers in-house alterations, find out if they guarantee the tailor's work. If not, consider hiring a freelance tailor. Tailoring can be very expensive and is sometimes a source of income for bridal shops.

- Allow four to six weeks, and several fittings, for alterations. Make sure the fittings are done with the undergarments and shoes you will wear for the wedding.
- If someone is sewing your gown, make sure she has plenty of time. Use only an experienced seamstress and remember to provide all the right notions along with an exact picture of what you want. Arrange several fittings at various stages, just to make sure.
- If your budget is tight, consider borrowing or renting a gown. Renting will generally save 40 to 60% of the cost of purchasing, but the selection will be limited. Make sure you understand the rental terms, including the store's policy for rental dress alterations, cleaning, delivery, and return. Be sure to get everything in writing.
- Ask for instructions on pressing and storing your gown before the wedding, and how your gown should be preserved after the wedding.
- Keep all your receipts.

TEMPLE-READY DRESSES

Most bridal gowns will need to be altered in some way if you plan to wear the dress for the temple ceremony. The temple does offer inserts to be placed under lace or sheer material, and sleeve extensions for dresses with short sleeves, to help dresses meet temple requirements. You may want to consider purchasing a separate temple dress to be married in that may be worn again each time you attend the temple. Or you may decide to use a dress supplied by the temple. All temples carry a selection of lovely wedding dresses that a bride may wear for the temple marriage ceremony without charge.

The following guidelines have been established for bridal gowns that are worn in the temple (*Ensign,* June 1997, p. 72):

- The dress must be white—not off-white, ivory, or cream. If you are in doubt about the fabric color, try holding a piece of white typing paper next to the dress or take a swatch of the fabric to the temple for approval. Lace and other ornamentation must also be white.

- Sheer fabric and lace must be lined. Camisoles and sleeve liners may be worn under a dress that has sheer areas or see-through lace panels.
- The dress must be full length. If the skirt has a slit up the side or back that exposes the leg, some kind of filler must be worn to fill the gap. Temple workers can provide a slip or back apron if the bride does not wish to furnish her own.
- Long sleeves are required. If your gown has short sleeves, special sleeve extensions (usually in the form of a satin, long-sleeved shirt worn under the dress) are available at temples throughout the world.
- The neckline and back must be high enough to cover garments. A piece of material similar to a dickey will be inserted if your dress shows the shoulder or collarbone.
- The train must be removable or be designed to gather into a bustle for the temple ceremony.
- A white bra, white slip, and white nylons will be required for the temple.
- In keeping with the sacred nature of the temple, dresses should be free of elaborate ornamentation, and jewelry should be simple and tasteful.

HEADPIECE AND/OR VEIL

There are many different styles of headpieces and many styles and lengths of veils. A headpiece may be worn separately or with a veil. Or you can wear a veil without a headpiece. The two pieces are usually sold separately.

The bridal gown itself will largely determine what headpiece and veil you wear, because they should match the style of the dress. You may want to try on traditional pieces, as well as various options to the traditional approach, such as hats, flower wreaths, or decorative hair accessories. Keep in mind how you will be wearing your hair on your wedding day, the shape of your face and forehead, and comfort and ease in wearing the headpiece and/or veil. If your reception will include dancing, you may want to consider a detachable veil.

The headpiece and veil are not worn for the temple marriage ceremony, but can be worn outside the temple for wedding photographs.

SLIP

The design of the gown you select will determine the style of slip required. Some dresses have a slip that is part of the dress; many require an additional slip. Many bridal shops will rent a slip for much less than the purchase price. Make sure you wear the slip you are going to wear with the dress for any fittings.

SHOES AND HOSE

Shoes are selected to match your wedding dress. Whether you choose heels or flats is a matter of personal preference. Consider your height and the height of your fiancé. Above all, make sure the shoes are comfortable, and don't forget to break them in before your wedding day.

White nylons are required for the temple, and most brides wear them for the reception as well. Many bridal shops have nylons with decorative printed flowers, pearls, or tiny ribbons at the ankle or up the side. You may want to buy a second pair of hose, just so you have a backup pair in case of a run.

JEWELRY

The jewelry you select should be simple and tasteful. Pearls, diamonds, and rhinestones are traditional favorites. Family heirlooms, if available and appropriate, are also a nice choice.

The tradition of "Something old, something new, something borrowed, something blue—and a lucky sixpence in your shoe!" can be implemented with jewelry, shoes, hose, or other accessories. You may wish to consider a new white hanky, a garter with a blue ribbon, earrings your mother or grandmother wore, and so on.

UNDERCLOTHING

A white bra and white slip will be required for the temple. Make certain these fit comfortably. You will need to take temple garments with you if you are being endowed on the day of the wedding.

BEAUTY TIPS

Hair and makeup is done the morning of the wedding. If you desire a manicure, it can be done a day or two before. Any or all of these will help you feel relaxed, ready, and beautiful for the most important day of your life. However, don't feel pressured to get your hair done or to have a manicure unless you want to. You will need to plan and schedule any of these appointments in advance.

There are no facilities for hairdressers at the temple. However, many salons offer a "touch up" for the bride, just preceding the reception. This may well be needed after the rigors of the day, especially if your hairstyle is at all elaborate or if you wish to change your daytime hairstyle to a different style for the evening reception.

Make arrangements well in advance and ask the following questions:
- What is the cost?
- Exactly what services will be provided?
- Where and when will we meet for the touch-up work?

Tips

Most hairdressers appreciate a picture of how you want your hair to look.

Consider meeting with the hairdresser in advance. Take your headpiece and veil with you so you can discuss different styling options.

If you wish to do something a little different and more exotic with either your hair or your makeup, experiment before the day of the wedding. It is well worth the cost to try out a new look ahead of time to see if it works for you.

Be cautious about a hairstyle that is so different from how you normally look that both you and your guests will feel uncomfortable (and you will not recognize the girl in the photos years from now).

If your budget allows, have a manicure—even from a friend. It will make you feel better.

Tasteful makeup is a definite enhancer of what the camera can do, but keep it natural enough that your true beauty shows through.

O love! Thine essence is thy purity!

—L. E. Landon

7
Groom's Attire

For all but the most informal wedding receptions, a tuxedo is the traditional attire for the groom. As a general rule, if the bride is wearing a street-length dress or suit, the groom should wear a dark business suit with a white dress shirt and tie. If the bride is wearing a full-length dress, the groom should wear a tuxedo. However, there are many styles of formal wear available for the groom. Be careful to keep in mind the style of your gown and the formality of your wedding reception in making this selection.

Basic Tuxedo Styles

- Semiformal: formal dinner jacket with matching trousers, white or colored dress shirt, optional cummerbund or vest, and black bow tie
- Formal: formal dinner jacket or cutaway jacket, matching trousers, waistcoat, white wing-collared shirt (tuxedo shirt), cummerbund or vest, black bow tie or ascot
- Very formal: cutaway jacket or tailcoat, matching striped trousers, white wing-collared shirt, waistcoat or vest, ascot or bow tie, and patent leather shoes

Shoes and Socks

Shoes should match the tuxedo in style and formality and may be rented at the tuxedo shop. Stockings should match the color of the trousers and shoes.

Hints and Helps

- Black is the preferred color for more formal receptions, regardless of the season of the year.
- For less formal receptions, consider darker colors such as gray in the fall or winter and lighter colors in the spring or summer.
- Select a reputable tuxedo shop.
- Ask if the tuxedo shop offers a discount on the groom's tuxedo if the other members of the wedding party rent their tuxedos at that shop.
- If the groom is living out of town prior to the wedding, his measurements can be taken at any tuxedo shop and called in to the shop from which the tuxedos will be rented.
- Formal wear should be reserved several weeks before the wedding to allow ample time for alterations. If possible, reserve tuxedos for the groom's attendants at the same time you reserve the groom's tuxedo.
- Plan to pick up the tuxedo a few days before the wedding and check the fit in case last-minute alterations are needed.
- Make sure you understand the store's return policy and arrange to have one of the groom's attendants return the tuxedo.
- Get everything in writing and keep your receipts.

8

WEDDING PARTY ATTIRE

Attire for the wedding party should match the style of the bride and groom. Clothing for attendants and parents usually reflect the color scheme of the wedding.

There are some practical guidelines that you can follow. After that, go with the flow. You may not be able to get exactly the tuxedos you wanted, or your mother-in-law may have a different idea about her dress than you did. Remember, people coming through your wedding line will not really notice exactly what everyone is wearing, as long as everyone looks nice. In the end, the bride should be the main attraction. Do what you can, and then relax.

BRIDE'S ATTENDANTS

Use the following general guidelines in selecting the wedding attire for the maid or matron of honor, bridesmaids, and flower girls.

- Coordinate the style of attendants' attire with the bride's, as much as possible.
- Attendants' dresses do not have to be identical. Often the maid of honor wears a slightly different style than the bridesmaids.
- Select a style that flatters a variety of figures.
- You may want to choose dresses that can be worn again for other occasions.

- Unless the bride and her family are covering the cost of the dresses, it is important to identify and stay within the budgets of the attendants.
- Keep accessories simple.
- Junior bridesmaids (roughly ages 10 to 16) can have differing dresses from the other bridesmaids or flower girls.
- Flower girl dresses may be long or short, and may either match or complement the other attendants' dresses.
- Try to order or purchase all dresses at the same time to lessen confusion, avoid color variances due to different dye lots, and possibly take advantage of any group discounts offered by the bridal shop.
- When shopping, be prepared with the dress sizes of all your attendants. Many stores carry samples or floor models only, so ask the staff to check the availability of your selection in all sizes needed before you make a final decision.
- While three to four weeks is an average delivery schedule, be aware that it can take up to several months. Ask about a delivery date before you place an order and make sure you allow time for any necessary alterations.
- If possible, attendants should try on their dresses before ordering to make sure that the style and fit are flattering. This will help minimize alteration costs. If an attendant lives out of town, see if the bridal shop will ask the manufacturer for a list of stores carrying that brand name in the attendant's hometown.
- Ask for an estimate of alteration costs before ordering.
- Be prepared to pay a sizable deposit, if not the entire sum, for the dresses at the time the order is placed.
- If the dresses will be hand-sewn, make certain to provide complete measurement information to the seamstress along with the names, ages, and phone numbers of each attendant. Be sure that attendants will be available for fittings before deciding on this option. Agree on a completion date and cost in advance.

- Allow plenty of time for hand-sewn dresses to be made so this does not become a source of distress to you or your attendants.
- Make sure you also coordinate shoes, hairstyles, makeup, jewelry, and other accessories of bridal attendants.
- Get everything in writing and keep all your receipts.

Groom's Attendants

Use the following general guidelines in selecting attire for the best man and groom's attendants.

- Coordinate the style of the attendants' attire with the groom, as much as possible.
- Out-of-town men in the wedding party can have their measurements taken at any tuxedo shop and called in to the shop from which the tuxedos will be rented.
- Reserve all tuxedos several weeks before the wedding to allow ample time for alterations.
- Plan to pick up the tuxedos a few days before the wedding and have each person try them on in case last-minute alterations are needed.
- Make sure you understand the store's return policy.
- Get everything in writing and keep your receipts.

Parents

Parents of the bride and groom often have strong feelings about their own attire for the wedding. Their opinions should be taken into consideration. Traditionally, the fathers should be in tuxedos if the groom is wearing a tuxedo, but a dark business suit with white dress shirt and tie is also acceptable. The mothers may wear formal street-length or full-length dresses that match or complement your wedding colors. Most mothers will want to wear a different, less formal dress for the temple ceremony and more formal attire for the reception. Make sure you communicate to the mothers what each is wearing to avoid the unlikely chance of their dresses being identical or clashing in some way.

I would rather have a crust and a tent with you than be queen of all the world.
> —Isabel to her husband, Richard Burton

9
GUEST LISTS

Begin to compile your guest list as early as possible. The bride and groom, the bride's parents, and the groom's parents should each make a list of the people they would like to invite, including their complete names (as they should appear on the invitation) and addresses. Determine ahead of time if you wish to include children. If so, the names of each child in the family should be included on the guest list.

To maximize efficiency as the lists are generated, indicate by each entry the events that the individual, couple, or family are invited to attend. (See worksheet for Master Guest List in the last chapter of this book.) Single adult guests age 18 and older should receive a separate invitation even if they are living with their parents. Be sure to indicate on the master list and on the invitation if single adults are invited to bring a guest. To get an accurate count, be sure to include everyone in the bride and groom's immediate family on the master list, as well as each attendant and his or her parents. Remember to double-check that names are spelled correctly and to verify addresses. Watch for duplication from various sources.

After the lists have been gathered, combine:
- family on both sides
- close family friends on both sides
- friends and associates of the bride and groom
- neighbors and parents' business associates
- old school friends, teachers, and previous business associates

These groupings will help you determine where any cuts should be made if the guest list exceeds your budget.

Once you have compiled a master list, make a permanent record for you and one for each family. You can copy and use the Master Guest List from the Charts and Worksheets chapter in this book, or select another method that works best for you such as:

- a computer list that you can easily add to, organize, and mark
- an address book in which you can check off names and jot notes
- cards kept in a file—one for each guest or family, with notations

Lists can often be used for future family weddings. Use your master list to develop at least two working lists—one for the temple marriage ceremony and one for the reception. If you plan to have a wedding breakfast, you will also want to create a separate guest list for that event. The master list can help determine how many announcements, invitations, and various enclosures you will need, as well as how those materials should be addressed. It will also provide a rough head count for selecting a reception site and obtaining catering estimates.

Tips

Set a deadline for completing the list.

If space and budget allow, include any people who perform services for you—hairdresser, tailor, cake decorator, etc. They may like to see their handiwork in its glory!

All true love is grounded on esteem.
— Buckingham

10

Announcements, Invitations, and Thank-You Notes

There are many places to shop for wedding announcements, invitations, and thank-you notes. You will also find a variety of styles and prices from which to choose. Printers and stationery stores have books you can look through. Many reception centers also offer invitations as part of their services. Brides can even create their own invitations with their word processors and laser printers. You can buy blank cards, papers, and stock envelopes in bulk in many different sizes and styles. This is less traditional, but can save on cost.

Remember to shop prices—it may make a big difference. Typically, however, the cost of the invitation will be determined by the quality of the paper and the type of printing. Engraving is the most expensive form of printing and the most formal in appearance. The paper is pressed onto a copper plate which raises the letters slightly from the page. Thermography, which may be used for either formal or informal invitations, is a commonly used technique that combines powder and ink to create the appearance of raised letters. It is approximately one-third the cost of engraved printing. Offset printing is the least expensive process and is also the least formal.

Wedding Announcements

Announcements are not essential, but can be useful to send to family, friends, and acquaintances who are not invited to the wedding or the reception either because the number of guests must be limited or because they live too far away. Announcements do not carry an obligation of sending a gift and should never be sent to anyone who has received an invitation to the temple marriage ceremony or the reception. They should be printed on the same paper and style as the invitations. Generally, the announcements are addressed before the wedding and mailed within a day or two after the event.

INVITATIONS

For Latter-day Saint weddings, the invitation is traditionally used to invite guests to the reception rather than the temple marriage ceremony. If desired, the invitation may also include an enclosure card for the sealing ceremony, a response card and self-addressed, stamped return envelope for a wedding brunch or luncheon, and a map. It is appropriate to indicate on the reception invitation if you are having more than one reception. This information can be placed in two columns at the bottom of the invitation, allowing guests to select the celebration most convenient for them to attend.

Traditional or Formal Invitations

A traditional style usually consists of an outer mailing envelope, an inner envelope, and the invitation itself. The wording for a traditional invitation is generally a more formal style than for a contemporary or informal invitation. The reception center or printer can provide you with standard wording for formal invitations. The invitation, along with any enclosures, should be placed in the inner envelope facing the back (or unaddressed side). Place the inner envelope with the guests' names facing the back (or unaddressed side) of the outer envelope.

Contemporary or Informal Invitations

The use of informal wedding invitations has become much more popular in recent years. Informal invitations can be a way to show the creative, personal style of the bride and groom. You may include a photo or photos, opt for a double- or triple-folded form requiring only one envelope, and word the information as you desire. Unusual papers, ribbons, and printing can be incorporated. In creating your own design, however, exercise caution and taste and check postal regulations for size and postage requirements.

ENCLOSURE CARDS

Enclosure cards are usually included for the purpose of inviting a select group of guests to the temple marriage ceremony. Be sure to include the name of the temple and the time guests will be required to arrive. (It may be a good idea to indicate a time 15 minutes prior to the arrival time specified by the temple, because latecomers may not be allowed to attend.) The enclosure card can also be used as an invitation to the wedding breakfast or luncheon, if desired. Or you may provide a separate enclosure card for the wedding breakfast or luncheon.

RESPONSE CARDS

Response cards are enclosed with the invitation when it is important to determine the exact number of people who will be attending. An invitation to the temple marriage ceremony does not usually require a response, but an invitation to the wedding breakfast or luncheon may require an exact head count for catering and seating arrangements. The response card should be placed in the invitation with a self-addressed, stamped return envelope.

MAPS

Consider including a map to the reception if the location will be difficult to find. Maps should be printed in a similar style to and on a similar or coordinating paper as the invitation; however, maps are often printed at a local copy center rather than with the invitations. Visual and/or written directions should be included.

THANK-YOU NOTES

Thank-you notes can be ordered with invitations and are often in the same style as a traditional or formal invitation. These must be hand-written and as personalized as possible, referring to the actual gift received. Regardless of whether the bride has thanked the giver in person, a written thank-you note is essential.

INVITATION CHECKLIST

- It is better to order too many of something than too few. Make a thorough guest list before settling upon a number and order up to 20% more stationary than your actual head count requires. Extras may be used as family keepsakes.
- Discuss and agree on the style, design, and wording before the invitations are ordered.
- As a courtesy to parents, discuss with them how they would like their names to appear.
- Take a sample of the invitation, along with any enclosure or response cards, to the post office and check the weight and postage amounts that will be required. Be aware that many invitations require additional postage.
- Specify paper stock, type font, and ink colors to be used for each piece of printed material and make sure that information is included on the order form.
- Ask the supplier for a proof of the material for you to double-check before the invitations are actually printed.
- A return address is required by the post office. This is usually the current address of the bride.

ADDRESSING THE INVITATIONS

There are several rules governing the proper way to address wedding invitations. The printer or reception center where you order your invitations will usually provide specific instructions. General guidelines are as follows:

Invitations to a Couple

The outer envelope should be addressed to Mr. and Mrs. (always spell out the word *and*), followed by the husband's first and last name. (Example: Mr. and Mrs. William Johnson.) The inner envelope should also be addressed to Mr. and Mrs., followed by the last name. (Example: Mr. and Mrs. Johnson.) If the couple are family or close personal friends, the inner envelope may be addressed with the first names of the couple. Do not use abbreviations in writing out the address. Spell out such words as *North, South, Street, Apartment,* and so on. Spell out the name of the state rather than using abbreviations.

Invitations to a Family

Invitations to a family should be addressed on the outer envelope in the same way as invitations to a couple. The inner envelope should also be addressed to Mr. and Mrs., followed by their last name and the names of any younger family members (in order of age) you wish to be included in the invitation. (Example: Mr. and Mrs. Johnson, Michael, Emily, and Peter.) Omitting children's names from the inner envelope infers that the children are not invited. Children over the age of 18 but still living at home should be sent a separate invitation.

Invitations to a Single Adult

The outer envelope should be addressed to Mr., Miss, Ms., or Mrs. (in the case of a widowed woman), followed by the first and last name of the individual. (Examples: Miss Susan Jones; Ms. Nancy Taylor; Mr. John Smith; Mrs. Mary White.) Drop the first name for the inner envelope, but specify "and Guest" if they may bring a partner. (Example: Miss Jones and Guest.) For family or close personal friends, it is permissible to use a first name only on the inner envelope.

- Do not slight or leave out parents, particularly in cases of divorce and blended families.
- If time is short, ask to receive envelopes earlier to begin addressing them.
- Have a party where "the girls" get together to address invitations, with good conversation, refreshments, or perhaps a video afterward.
- Carry several unaddressed invitations around with you. You will undoubtedly find yourself running into old school friends, teachers, or perhaps someone you forgot. It will be a delight to make contact, tell them of your upcoming wedding, and pull out an announcement or invitation right there.
- Gather an eclectic array of thank-you notes to send for showers and reception gifts. It doesn't matter if the notes don't match, as long as they reflect your personality.

With such ardent eyes he wandered o'er me, and gazed with such intensity of love . . . sending his soul out to me in a look.

—Young

11

PHOTOGRAPHY AND
WEDDING VIDEO

Photographs are the most permanent keepsake of your wedding day. They are tangible proof of your beauty and happiness on the day you were joined with your husband forever. Photographs from your wedding will be cherished by you and future generations. If possible, reserve a photographer with wedding experience as early as possible in the planning stage. Select a photographer whose style reflects the kind of photographs you want. Discuss with the photographer the type and number of pictures you and your fiancé have in mind before obtaining an estimate for services. Be aware that the cost of photographs in addition to those in your wedding package will be an additional expense.

Many couples also opt to have a wedding video. Professional videographers will come to the temple grounds and the reception to put together a video for you. Or you may choose to have a family member or close friend videotape your wedding for you. Photography and videography can be a big expense. Look closely at what you want most and prioritize accordingly.

ENGAGEMENT PICTURE

This picture can be in either a formal or casual setting. Some couples like to take both formal and casual pictures. The engagement photo may be included with announcements or invitations. A copy of the picture is often displayed at the wedding reception.

Bridal Portrait

The bridal portrait is taken of the bride in her wedding gown as soon as the dress is ready, preferably a month or two before the wedding. This picture is also often displayed at the wedding reception. Sometimes a bridal bouquet is created specifically for the photograph; if not, photographers generally have several silk bridal bouquets to choose from for the picture.

Wedding Day Photographs

Photographs on the wedding day are usually taken on the temple grounds following the ceremony or occasionally right before the ceremony. In addition, photographs are also taken before and during the reception.

Wedding Video

Your imagination is the limit as far as moving pictures are concerned. Often a prewedding video of the bride and groom is played continuously during the reception. Entrust this task to someone both creative and reliable. Provide written instructions and feel free to give suggestions. Ask to see a sample of the videographer's work before making a commitment.

You will also want a video recording of your wedding day events. Professional videographers can also be hired for this. Or find someone within your scope of friends or family who owns and will run a top-grade video recorder for you. Again, be specific about what you want.

Tips

Make a written list of specific poses or people you want to have photographed, and discuss it with your photographer.

Discuss with the photographer how much time to allow for photographs both at the temple and before the reception.

12

FLOWERS

Flowers are an important part of a wedding. They add romance to any gathering, especially a wedding. Depending on the flowers you choose, they can set the mood as formal and elegant or more casual and playful. You and your groom must determine, based on your preestablished budget, whether flowers will be a modest, minimal part of your wedding, or more lavishly and richly done.

FLOWERS FOR THE WEDDING PARTY

- The bride should choose, and communicate to the groom, what she wants her bouquet to look like.
- The groom's boutonniere should be different from the boutonnieres worn by his attendants or other members of the wedding party.
- The maid of honor usually has a little larger or slightly different bouquet than the bridesmaids.
- Flowers for the bride's attendants should coordinate with their dresses and the color scheme for the wedding. If possible, take a swatch of fabric to the florist with you.
- Flower girls may wear wreaths of flowers on their heads and/or carry a basket of flower petals.

- You may want to make arrangements to have the flowers for the wedding party delivered to the temple grounds by a family member or friend for photograph taking.
- Ask your florist about preserving your flowers after the wedding.

Tips

Shop around, comparing samples, styles, and prices.

Ask friends who have recently married about their experience with their florist.

Bring a list with you, so you don't forget anything or anyone, and the florist can make an accurate price estimate.

Use flowers that are in season.

Ask about delivery and set-up charges.

Arrange enough time for setting up the flowers at the reception site. Also arrange for someone to be there when the flowers are delivered.

Arrange for someone to take home the flowers from the reception and keep, recut, enjoy, or preserve them while you are on your honeymoon.

Using potted plants or silk flowers is also an option.

The accents of Love are all that is left of the language of paradise.

—Bulwer

13

THE WEDDING CAKE

A wedding cake may be any size or shape. The cake should reflect your wedding colors or theme, and your own personal style. Cake flavor is no longer limited to vanilla and chocolate, so pick anything you like. The wedding cake is typically displayed on its own table. You may also want to consider a groom's cake, which is a smaller cake, usually (but not always) displayed next to the wedding cake at the reception.

The size of the cake you order should be determined by:

- how many guests you intend to serve.
- whether the cake will be used as part of the refreshment food for the evening.
- if you will include a cake-cutting ceremony as part of your festivities.
- if you want to save the top portion of the cake to freeze and be brought out for your first anniversary celebration.

Tips

Shop around and look at photos and actual examples of bakers' previous work, if possible. Explain what you want, carefully and in writing, to make certain they can comply.

Get costs in writing. Even if the baker will provide only an estimate range, pin down that range with all the details of your specifications to avoid misunderstandings.

Discuss delivery charges and any extra fees for set-up.

Define terms for any plates, pillars, or other decorative elements that need to be returned.

Consider decorating your cake with fresh flowers. These can be ordered from the baker or the florist, or you may have a friend or family member who would like to help. In any case, make sure the floral arrangement you desire is understood, and agree on a price in advance for the flowers to be used.

Love is the crowning grace of humanity . . . the Holiest right of the Soul.

—Petrarch

14

REGISTERING FOR GIFTS

Most couples choose to register for gifts. It is a good way to give people ideas about what you would like, and it is nice for you to get some of the presents that you particularly wanted. Of course, you will always enjoy many gifts that are a surprise, but it is nice to give guests a starting place for shopping.

It is possible to register in a variety of stores, from mass market superstores to the most exclusive china, silver, and kitchen shops. Decide what suits you and prioritize your needs. You can register for everything from china to designer bathroom fixtures; from linen to art for your walls.

Register as early as possible, at least a month before the wedding—earlier if you want the information to be used for showers as well. Take time to walk through the stores together, selecting a variety of items from a wide price range. It will be enjoyable for you and your fiancé to pick out the things you want to make your home together. After all, you might as well get the towels that match your bathroom, rather than others you may need to trade in.

Most stores have an easy procedure for registering. The store will provide a form or a bar code scanner for you to select as many items as you desire. As your guests come in to purchase a gift, they can access the information and find out which items on your list have been purchased already. This provides for very little guesswork and very little duplication.

Update your gift registry as you see or think of new items you would like to include. You may want to check it yourself, especially after showers, to see if you need more selections for actual wedding gift purchases when the time comes. Before registering, be sure to check store policies, particularly with regard to returns and exhanges. Some stores will offer only a store credit for returns. On the other hand, many stores offer a 10% or 20% discount on wedding list items that you purchase yourself during the first three months following the wedding.

It is appropriate to indicate to guests the stores where the bridal couple are registered. Some families feel it is most appropriate to provide this information only when asked; many others feel it is perfectly acceptable to include this information on the wedding invitation or as an enclosure.

Hints and Helps

- If you have many friends or family members from out of town or out of state, consider registering at stores that are nationwide. Most national stores have a computerized registry service that is interconnected with all of their locations.
- Register at more than one store to give a wider price choice to your guests.
- Keep a copy of your wedding registry for your own records.

We are shaped and fashioned by what we love.
—Goethe

15

SHOWERS AND PARTIES

Marriage is a time for celebration! Parties will start soon after your engagement and the celebration will continue through your wedding day.

ENGAGEMENT PARTY

This is a delightful custom that has largely fallen into disuse, most probably due to the shorter engagement periods of today's couples. Such parties are usually hosted by the bride's parents and limited to immediate family members and close friends. The format may be informal, with the invitations handwritten or merely verbal.

Traditionally, the official announcement is made at the engagement party, and tributes are given to the prospective bridal couple, beginning with the father of the bride and responded to by the groom. If you choose to have an engagement party, implement your own customs and celebrate the occasion as seems fitting to you.

BRIDAL SHOWERS

A variety of showers are often given for the bride, by the bride's family, the groom's family, friends, coworkers, or the Relief Society. These showers are commonly hosted by a best friend, aunt, cousin, sister, future sister-in-law, coworker, or close family friend. Accommodate your family and friends by telling them what you want and providing information about guest lists, colors, styles, preferences, and needs.

It is customary to have a family shower given by the bride's family, the groom's family, or jointly. Depending on the size of the family and the location of family members, immediate members of both families—mothers, sisters, and grandmothers—are usually invited to these gatherings. This helps to break the ice and introduce the members of each family to one another.

Hostesses of bridal showers often like to have a theme such as:
- kitchen shower
- bathroom shower
- linens shower
- personal shower
- food shower
- holiday shower

Tips

Provide any information or materials you are asked for as promptly and cheerfully as possible.

Be gracious. Greet guests and express appreciation for their kindness.

Be on time.

List showers and shower gifts in one central notebook (such as in the pages provided at the back of this planner).

Send thank-you notes as soon as possible, checking them off as they are sent. It will be extremely helpful to you to have the shower acknowledgments taken care of before the wedding day.

Prepare special thank-yous for the hostess of each shower.

Some families choose to have a special family temple night that can add a beautiful spiritual dimension to the prewedding festivities. You may want to do this when you take out your own endowment, if you have not done so before (see chapter 3). Some families like to attend a temple session together on the day of the wedding.

This night can be a small and intimate gathering, or may be expanded to include a large number of family members who want to share this moment with you. The decision is yours, but structure the events of the day or evening so the Spirit of the Lord can be present to bless you and crown the experience with as few distractions and outside demands as possible.

Tips

You may wish to organize a luncheon or dinner following the temple session to give family members a chance to visit.

Ask a member of your group to take photographs of you and your fiancé outside the temple, if desired.

Make sure you and your fiancé have some time alone together, either before or after the temple session, and write about it in your journal before you go to bed that night.

We attract hearts by those qualities we display: we retain them by the qualities we possess.

—Suard

16

THE WEDDING DAY

The big day is finally here! The following are a few suggestions that may help keep you centered on one of the most important days of your life. As you go through this day, remember the temple sealing ordinance should be the center and focus of your celebration. Everything else is icing on the cake!

BRIDE'S SCHEDULE

- Be certain you know the hour when you are to arrive at the temple. Be on time! Be early, if possible.
- If you are having your hair styled before you go to the temple, provide ample time so that you will enjoy the experience and preparation, rather than feeling hurried and stressed.
- Make specific travel arrangements. Will you be driving with your parents? With the groom? Who is meeting whom, exactly where and exactly when?
- Make time for both personal and family prayer, with your parents, with your groom, or both.

ITEMS TO BRING TO THE TEMPLE

- your marriage license
- your special temple recommend for a live sealing
- a nice white handkerchief or two, if desired

- your temple clothes, if you have them, and garments to wear afterward
- the groom's temple clothes and garments in a separate bag
- any makeup, jewelry, or personal items you wish to have, either for the temple or for pictures afterward
- wedding dress, shoes, and accessories in a separate bag
- the groom's tuxedo, shoes, and accessories in a separate bag
- emergency kit consisting of aspirin and stomach aid, breath spray or mints, clear nail polish, deodorant, tissues, extra nylons, safety pins, hair pins, curling iron, sewing kit, spot remover, toothbrush, and toothpaste

If you wish to carry a bridal bouquet for pictures after the sealing ceremony, arrange for the florist or a member of your party who is not attending the temple marriage ceremony to deliver the flowers for you. The temple workers will be happy to keep the flowers for you until you are ready for them.

Schedule for Participants

It is very helpful for all members of the wedding party, as well as close family and friends, to have a written schedule for the day's events. Be sure everyone involved has the following information:

- Make arrival time for temple guests clear. (Follow temple instructions for determining the amount of time temple guests will need to arrive before the ceremony.)
- Specify an arrival time for members of your party who are coming for photographs following the temple marriage ceremony, but not to the ceremony itself.
- Make arrangements for any children who will need to be transported and attended to at the temple.
- Designate an exact time for the wedding breakfast or luncheon, especially for those who will not be in attendance at the temple.
- Designate an exact time for family and other participants to arrive for the reception. Include ample time for wedding photographs to be taken before the celebration begins.

- Review the Wedding Checklist in the Charts and Worksheets chapter at the back of this book. Check for people with special assignments. Make certain each person knows the specific details of what, where, and when.

Tip
Place a reliable person (mother, sister, friend) in charge of general reminding and arranging. You will be glad you did.

THE TIME BETWIXT AND BETWEEN

After the temple ceremony, you may have pictures, a wedding breakfast, and later in the day a reception. Even with the festivities, you may be fortunate and find yourself with a breathing space between events and demands. If you are tired, take a moment to put your feet up. If there is something left undone, now is the time to tie up loose ends. Most of your wedding party will find themselves as busily scheduled as you are. If some of your guests are from out of town, you may wish to provide ideas of local points of interest, which they may wish to visit during this time.

KEEPING IT SPIRITUAL

- You may want your father, grandfather, bishop, fiancé, or someone else you especially love and trust to give you a blessing either the morning of your wedding or sometime in the last days preceding it. Perhaps you and your fiancé can arrange special family blessings together, from both fathers, with both mothers present.
- Close your eyes and utter a little prayer of gratitude. Remember the great blessings of the temple, and of being united for time and all eternity with the one you love. Let your happiness show.

Stress on your wedding day cannot be avoided. But there are things which might help.

- Have a professional massage the week, or a few days, before the wedding. If possible, a skilled sister, brother, or roommate might give a massage the night before, or in the time between the ceremony and reception. Neck, shoulders, and feet are places of special stress. Concentrate on these.

- If you have a headache, rub lavender oil on your wrists and temples several times throughout the day. It works.

- Depending upon your own personality and preferences, try to catch a catnap—even if for only fifteen minutes—at some point during the day. Or simply stretch out, close your eyes, and breathe deeply for a minute or two. Chances are that you did not get sufficient sleep the night before the wedding, or for many nights before that! These little breaks will make a big difference.

- If it helps you to play soothing music, try to arrange this. Or if quiet helps, just five minutes alone in a darkened room will make a difference you will appreciate as the evening wears on.

- Don't eat too much—or too little—but try to drink a lot of water to keep hydrated.

Love one human being purely and warmly, and you will love all.

—Richter

17

WEDDING BREAKFAST OR
LUNCHEON

The wedding breakfast or luncheon can be a lovely and memorable event. There is a sense of intimacy you share on your wedding day with this smaller group of those who are so close to you.

This event is the responsibility of the groom's family, but usually the bride and groom will be allowed to choose both the location and the menu.

- It is customary to invite everyone who attends the sealing ceremony in the temple, as well as other family members and close friends, to the wedding breakfast. All members of the wedding party should be included.
- Try to find a location for the event in close proximity to the temple.
- Determine if any of your guests have special dietary needs. These needs usually can be accommodated if they are requested in advance.

SCHEDULING CONSIDERATIONS

It is quite difficult to determine precisely how long after the marriage ceremony to plan the wedding breakfast or luncheon. After the temple photographs have been taken, you will need to change clothes and freshen up a bit, and allow time for visiting among friends and family. Discuss with your photographer how much time he or she will need for both family photographs and individual shots of the bride and groom. Make ample provision for this. If your guests have an hour to wait before the breakfast or luncheon is scheduled, they can find ways to fill it.

PROTOCOL

Since the affair is generally hosted by the groom's parents, the groom's father usually takes charge at the event. Many couples prefer a simple welcome and prayer by the father; others like a program or a time for guests to give advice to the bride and groom. Plan beforehand how you want the breakfast or luncheon to go. The groom's parents may want to:

- greet guests as they arrive.
- welcome the wedding couple and make acknowledgments.
- select someone to offer a prayer on the food.
- announce any program, speeches, or entertainment that has been planned, including tributes to (or memories of) the bride and groom by parents, siblings, or close friends; toasts made to the bridal couple; meaningful songs that will be performed; or serious or humorous advice to the new couple offered by the guests.

Tips

Keep any program or entertainment short and manageable. Know in advance how much time has been allotted and be careful to stay within that schedule.

Keep comments and entertainment appropriate for the wedding celebration.

SEATING ARRANGEMENTS

It is customary to have a head table at which the bride and groom, parents of the bride and groom, and grandparents (if space allows) are seated. This works well if there are a number of large round tables. If there are several long tables instead, the bride's party may occupy one table and the groom's party another. Sometimes place cards are utilized, so you can plan a safe or stimulating arrangement of your guests. Place children alongside responsible adults, or together at a separate table. Or, you can be random and trust to natural selection and chance.

Hints and Helps

- You may wish to personalize decorations with centerpieces, flowers, plants, ribbons, candles, and so on. Determine in advance what the restaurant will provide in the way of decoration and what they will allow to be brought in.
- You may wish to display photos of the bride and groom. Decide in advance how and where they will be displayed.
- Consider a separate guest book with room for guests to sign their names and give wedding advice to the bridal couple.
- If you plan to give special favors to the guests, make arrangements with the restaurant and assign someone else to oversee the details. (See chapter 18 for ideas for party favors.)

Wedding Dinner

Rather than a wedding breakfast or luncheon after the temple ceremony, some couples opt to have a wedding dinner the night before. A lovely sit-down dinner the evening before the wedding gives everyone a chance to catch their breath as they await the next day's events. It also frees up time on the actual wedding day so the couple's schedule is not jam-packed and they are not completely exhausted by the end of the evening.

18

WEDDING RECEPTION

The style and format of the reception should reflect the personality and desires of the bridal couple. Create your own style. Follow lovely wedding traditions, or alter traditional elements to suit your tastes and needs. Indeed, a reception itself is an optional thing.

If you choose a wedding reception, as a starting point consider the following conventional options:

- A reception held in a reception center, home, chapel, or garden. This usually includes a traditional receiving line, refreshments, and music or entertainment.
- An open house on a more casual level, where the bride and groom and other members of the wedding party mingle, rather than forming a formal receiving line. Light refreshments are usually served.
- A formal or semi-formal dinner for a smaller, more intimate number of wedding guests. A reception line might be observed at the beginning of the evening, followed by dancing after the meal.

Most of the information in this chapter pertains to a more traditional reception for an LDS wedding.

Reception Centers and Caterers

The food is typically the largest expense of the reception. The menu may be simple or sumptuous, according to your budget and style. There are many, many options to consider, and the price will vary widely between individual caterers and reception centers. Even if your engagement is short and your demands many, it is worthwhile to comparison shop for such essential wedding services.

Some reception centers handle the food entirely, giving you choices in menu selection, but not allowing any additional food (other than the wedding cake) to be brought in. Other reception sites will give you a list of approved caterers from which to choose. Check the policy carefully for each reception site you consider and factor in all applicable costs before making a decision.

Caterers have a set formula they use to help determine, based on the number of guests you have invited, how much food you will need. However, most caterers use a buffet-style service, so if you intend to have a program or dancing, you should plan for the reality that some guests will fill their plates more than once. This applies doubly to drinks.

Important Questions

- Does the caterer provide servers, or will you be required to provide your own servers?
- Does the caterer or reception center provide tables, chairs, linens, centerpieces, serving pieces, and dishes? Are the available items acceptable to you?
- What is the caterer's policy with regard to deposits, cancellations, and refunds?
- When will you have access to the site for delivery and set up of flowers, the wedding cake, music, and so on?
- If the location is outdoors, what contingencies are made for inclement weather?

ALTERNATIVES

Reception centers, hotels, and country clubs can be quite expensive, but there are a number of alternatives that may be considered:

- Eliminate the expense of a wedding reception and use the money for your honeymoon or to help buy a new home or cover other expenses.
- Consider a home or garden reception. Longtime favorites, they offer a warm, personal atmosphere.
- Don't feel limited by others' expectations. Eliminating the traditional wedding party and receiving line can save time and money, and focus attention on the bride and groom.
- Limit your guest list to the people who matter most. Invite family and close friends to the wedding breakfast or luncheon in lieu of a traditional reception.

HINTS AND HELPS

- Plan for more, rather than less, food. You don't want to be embarrassed by running out!
- Finalize all details on paper and make exact arrangements for time and set-up, especially if the reception is elaborate or in a yard.
- If you have a home or church reception and do the food yourself, make sure the mothers are not so involved that they cannot enjoy and be part of the wedding day. Plan simply and delegate as much as possible, but make sure that whoever assumes the responsibility is capable of handling and executing what you have planned.
- Create a sketch of the reception site to help you organize the arrangement of tables, flowers, decorations, lighting, music, and so on.

Transportation and Parking

Plan ahead for transportation to and from the reception site for out-of-town relatives and family members with special needs. It may be helpful to create a list of important guests who will need help with transportation and appoint family members to arrange for this service.

Parking is usually provided by the reception center. However, guests should be notified on the reception invitation or map of any special parking regulations. For a home or garden reception, you will want to take precautions and plan ahead.

Tips

Inform neighbors of the event and request their patience and cooperation for those few hours, perhaps asking if they wouldn't mind parking their own vehicles in driveways and garages rather than along the street.

Make sure family cars that will not be in use are parked elsewhere for the evening.

Assign someone to aid and direct guests.

Decoration and Decor

The decoration or theme for your reception will be determined largely by the site you select, the time of year, and your personal taste. For example, an outdoor setting may provide a "natural" theme without much additional decoration, while a Christmas wedding would most likely include traditional holiday decor.

Your flowers and wedding cake will be a large part of the decor for your wedding reception (see chapters 12 and 13). Keep this in mind as you plan for additional decorations.

Almost any theme can be worked into wedding decor. This could include traditional or cultural elements, personal interests, or seasonal motifs. Simple or elaborate, the more the theme reflects you, the better.

Traditional Decorating Ideas

- candles and strings of tiny, white lights
- balloons and bubbles
- hearts and ribbons
- ice sculptures and fountains
- live trees, plants, small ponds, or pools

Cultural Decorating Ideas

  To reflect your cultural heritage, consider one of the following:
- Asian theme, with coordinating food, music, and decor
- Scottish theme, with bagpipes, plaids, kilts, and traditional Scottish dances
- Irish green with shamrocks, Celtic designs, and Celtic music
- Traditional German fest with folk costumes and German music and food
- Polynesian luau with traditional food and entertainment
- Country flavor with a barbeque menu and country western band

Personal Interests

- old family photos and memorabilia
- a theme special to you, such as roses, bees, butterflies, birds, or angels
- period decoration: the Fifties, Roaring Twenties, or Victorian

THE RECEPTION LINE

Though some find a formal receiving line too structured, it is nice to stand together to greet those people who care enough to pause in their own busy lives to share this moment with you. This practice is also appreciated by those who would like to meet the side of the family they don't know yet, visually connecting brothers, sisters, and parents all together, and by those who haven't seen you or your family for ages and may not recognize family members in an unstructured setting.

It is not necessary to keep the receiving line in place for the entire reception. Some brides have a reception line at the beginning of the wedding and time for mingling with guests at the end.

Other brides choose to not have a formal receiving line at all. This gives the opportunity for real visiting which cannot take place in the crowded demands of a line. It also frees guests from standing in line for an hour or longer to offer their congratulations. A more formal reception, however, should include a wedding line.

The standard receiving-line order for LDS weddings, from left to right, is as follows:

- mother of the bride
- father of the bride
- mother of the groom
- father of the groom
- groom
- bride
- maid of honor
- best man
- bridesmaids

Another acceptable way is to have the best man stand between the groom and the father of the groom.

When no attendants are present, it is common for the bride's parents to stand to the left of the bridal couple, next to the bride, with the groom's parents at the right of the bridal couple, next to the groom. This is a popular way of having receiving lines—with only the bride and groom and their parents. The bride's and groom's attendants are still dressed in their formal wedding attire, but are free to mingle throughout the evening.

MUSIC

Music can do much to enhance the mood and romance of your night. Whether it plays a subtle or lively part in the celebration is up to you. You may very likely have friends you can call upon in various musical capacities. If not, professionals can usually be found for hire at reasonable prices, especially if you are in an area where there is a college or university with groups of young performers who want opportunities to work and make their abilities known.

Music can be used in the background throughout the reception or can be featured as part of a program. Dancing at the end of the evening is also enjoyable.

Background Music

- classical recordings
- chamber music ensemble
- harpist or pianist

Performing Music

- soloists (vocalists or musical instrument)
- trios
- small bands (particularly when coordinating with a specific cultural theme)

Dance Music

- prerecorded compilation of your favorite pieces
- small jazz or general performance bands
- professional DJ

PROGRAMS OR ENTERTAINMENT

Some couples like to plan a program or entertainment as part of their wedding reception. This is not required. If you do have entertainment, you may want to schedule it midway through the evening, so a good number of guests will be in attendance. Another way is to have the "party" near the very end of the night, after the formalities of a receiving line or dinner have concluded, and time is a bit more flexible.

Some suggestions for entertainment include:

- vocal selections—perhaps "your song" performed by a friend.
- live band pieces, especially if friends or family are involved.
- classical solo performances on the violin, harp, or piano.
- dance performances, especially from a particular culture or part of your theme.
- songs from other lands performed in native tongues.

Tips

Indicate on the reception invitation if a program will begin at a specific time.

Ask someone in advance to be master of ceremonies so you can sit back, relax, and enjoy.

Prepare printed programs for guests to follow along with and keep as a wedding remembrance.

Send a small gift and a note of thanks to unpaid performers. Prepare these before the wedding.

GUEST REGISTRY

Do not overlook the important little detail of a guest book. Choose any size or style you desire and place it on a table near the entrance of the reception site with a quill pen for signing names, and perhaps some flowers at the table.

GIFTS

- Appoint gift receivers to graciously take gifts from guests at the door, or to direct them to the location where gifts are to be placed.
- Provide ample space for the keeping of gifts. A small table

spilling over with presents, stuffed and piled haphazardly on top of each other, is both unattractive and inefficient.

- Make arrangements in advance for the people who will gather and transport your gifts to a central location, awaiting your return from the honeymoon. This task often can be assigned to the groom's attendants.

PARTY FAVORS

If time and budget will allow, it is lovely to provide a small remembrance for your guests to take home. Have these prepared and ready well in advance, making sure you have enough for everyone. Favors can be passed out to guests as they leave or placed at individual place settings on tables. If the favors are set out in a basket for guests to help themselves, you may want to include a sign indicating "Take one, please" and expressing your appreciation to your friends and guests.

Party favors might include:
- small containers of bubbles
- sachets
- votive candles
- dried flower bunches tied with ribbon
- card stock copies of a favorite poem or song
- tiny boxes with a bonbon, mint, or other treat tucked within
- fresh or dried lavender bunches
- very small containers of homemade lotion or cologne
- small bars of homemade scented soaps

TRADITIONS

There is something almost comforting in knowing that a practice or tradition has been around for a long, long time—that brides for hundreds of years have done the same things you are doing and most likely felt many of the same things you are feeling at those moments.

It gives you a link with other women whose most precious hopes and dreams were very like your own.

Cutting the Cake

The age-old custom of cutting the wedding cake together represents the bride and groom's first time "breaking bread" together as a married couple. It signifies their willlingness to share all their worldly goods with each other. The cake is usually cut near the end of the festivities, with much fanfare.

Tips

Don't forget a cake knife for cutting and serving.

Be mature. Enjoy the romance of feeding the cake to one another instead of smashing it in each other's faces.

If you are serving the cake as part of the refreshments, determine whether you will need a person to do the serving, and whether plates and forks will be provided.

Assign someone to remove, package, and take home the top layer of the cake if you plan to save it for your first anniversary celebration.

Throwing the Bouquet

Custom dictates that the single women at the celebration gather in the center of the floor near the bride, who throws the bouquet over her shoulder to the waiting group. Many brides choose to use a "toss bouquet" for this tradition, and save their actual bridal bouquet for preservation.

Tossing the Garter

If you decide to wear a fancy garter round one of your legs, it is customary for the groom to remove the garter and toss or fling it over his shoulder to a group of single men. If there is dancing, tradition holds that the man who catches the garter dances with the girl or woman who caught the bride's bouquet.

Throwing Rice

In many locations, throwing rice at the departing couple is no longer allowed because the grains of rice are considered harmful to birds and other wildlife. Check with the reception site to determine if throwing rice is allowed. If not, you can substitute birdseed, a mixture of sweet-smelling herbs, or flower petals (either fresh or dried), or blow bubbles.

GIFT BASKET

It is a thoughtful custom for a special friend or family member to prepare a basket of goodies for the departing couple. The basket may contain:

- bread and cheeses
- specialty drinks
- chocolates
- tins of gourmet foods
- lotions or bubble bath
- linen napkins
- candles

The bride and groom can enjoy this basket of goods on their wedding night.

THE GETAWAY

Find a chance to say your last good-byes and thank-yous before making your exit. Most brides will want to change out of their wedding gowns before leaving. Where you are headed will determine what you will wear. Don't go too grubby or too casual. You still want to look and feel beautiful on your wedding day.

Make sure you have a car arranged and waiting. It should be clean, filled with gas, the keys in your possession, and so on. Some couples borrow or rent a fancy sports car or have a limousine waiting for them on this occasion.

Tips

If you belong to a family that would be tempted to "decorate" your vehicle, and that is not agreeable to you, make sure only a few trusted people know where the car is hidden and waiting. Perhaps someone can bring it round when the time comes for you to leave.

If you hire a limousine to carry you from the reception to your destination, make sure you are ready at the appointed time or be prepared to pay extra for the driver's wait.

In many cities nostalgic horse-drawn carriages will take you right to the door of your hotel, or merely on a sweet moonlit drive before you retire for the evening.

Love in marriage should be the accomplishment of a beautiful dream, and not, as it too often is, the end.

—Karr

19

THE HONEYMOON

After all of the planning and anticipation of your wedding day is over, you are alone together at last.

WEDDING NIGHT ACCOMMODATIONS

Reserve wedding night accommodations well in advance. If you are leaving on a flight the following morning, you may want to stay somewhere close to the airport. Get a special room for your wedding night, one that both you and your fiancé like. Whether you are in a fancy hotel suite, a charming bed and breakfast, or a cabin hideaway, most places often offer wedding night specials. Discuss options at length with your fiancé, so that you are both in agreement and know what you are getting ahead of time.

Tips

Most hotels will let you look at the rooms before making your reservations.

Check out the bridal suite and make selections that please both you and your budget.

If the beauty and coziness of a bed and breakfast appeal to you, as they do to many, keep in mind that you may have less privacy in such a setting (especially if you marry in a busy season).

Mountain cabins are available in many areas. They may be a bit pricey, but discounts are often available depending on the season and day of the week.

Where to Go?

Where you go on your honeymoon is a big decision. Make sure you and your fiancé plan together somewhere you would both like to go. Maybe you would rather go somewhere more expensive for fewer days, or maybe you would prefer a longer stay in a more affordable setting. If you plan far enough in advance, you can take advantage of specials for travel and accommodations.

Some grooms like to plan the honeymoon as a surprise for their bride. If you are uncomfortable with this option, be sure to tell your fiancé, so you can plan your trip together.

Checklist for Packing

- Write out everything you will need, then check off items as you pack them.
- Have bags packed as well in advance as possible. This is one thing you can set aside—emotionally and practically—as taken care of and done.
- Make sure you include all the little things you would be sorry to do without: toothbrush, your favorite lotion, brush, comb, pins for your hair, your favorite shampoo, plenty of stockings and undergarments, a bag for soiled clothing, and so on.
- Check with your groom to make certain he has organized and packed what he will need.
- Don't forget a camera and sufficient film.

20

AFTER THE HONEYMOON

Now the real adventure begins! Hopefully, you will have arranged things well beforehand so that you know where you are going and what to expect once you arrive.

A PLACE TO LIVE

You will need to find, secure, and often place a deposit on a place to live after the wedding. Most couples will rent an apartment or a house for their first home, though older couples may be in a position to buy a house or condominium. Be certain you know the exact date you wish to take possession, and what the terms and conditions will be.

Secure living quarters as early as possible and gain permission to make changes to suit you, such as repairs, painting, or selection of curtains and fixtures. Once you know where you will be living, it will be easier to pick coordinated towels, bedspreads, items for the kitchen counters, and so on. If you are fortunate, this can be done before the wedding. If not, perhaps parents or siblings will agree to fix things up while the two of you are away, so that you have a home ready to receive you when you arrive. If that is not a possibility, it will still be an exciting adventure to work together—really together—to build your new home.

When selecting a place to live, be sure to ask such questions as:

- Who is responsible for paying for water, electricity, gas, and garbage pick-up?
- Who is responsible for yard care?
- What repairs need to be made, and who is responsible for making them?
- What parking facilities are available?
- What deposits are required? First month's rent? Last month's rent? Cleaning deposit? Utility deposits?
- Are pets allowed?

MOVING ARRANGEMENTS

Conditions and demands for moving will vary greatly. Maybe you are moving just around the corner. Maybe you are moving to his town or state, or to someplace new altogether. Maybe time constraints and schedules will get in the way and give you some headaches. Your best hope is the same as always: plan ahead. Do as much as you can, then relax and let the rest work itself out. After all, the two of you are together at last. It would be foolish to let the ups and downs of life spoil that.

Tips

Check on times, schedules, and deposits for moving vehicles as far in advance as you can.

If you are moving a short distance, large U-Haul trucks can be rented for a nominal daily fee, which will make your work much faster and easier.

STORAGE

If you can store things in your grandma's basement or your parents' garage, great! If not, look into the price of storage units, even if for a brief time. All your past lives will be crammed into bags and boxes You will have to decide what to do with them.

Type labels to tape on each box, telling exactly what that box contains.

Grade the contents of each box:
- "A" is essential (I need it right now).
- "B" is important (I would like to have it now).
- "C" is not quite so essential (I want it, but I don't need it now).
- "D" is childhood things (I want it, but I need it stored for awhile, until I have my own home and children).

NECESSARY LEGALITIES

Typically brides take their husband's last name. However, some brides today continue to go by their maiden names or choose to hyphenate their two last names. Make certain you are consistent with whatever name you choose, and always go by and sign the same name.

You will need to change your name on the following:
- driver's license
- ward and stake records
- car registrations
- social security card
- voter registration
- bank accounts
- credit cards
- leases or property titles
- insurance policies
- school or employment records
- post office name and address change forms

Tips

Some agencies require a copy of the marriage license to be sent along with name-change forms.

Some agencies and businesses can be notified by simply indicating a name change on monthly statement or bill.

Make sure your marriage certificate gets filed with the state.

THANK-YOU NOTES

Thoughtful thank-you notes are essential, no matter how difficult it may be to write and send them.

Here are some guidelines that may help you:

- A separate note should be written for shower and wedding gifts.
- Each note should be handwritten.
- Notes should be signed by only one person, but you can mention your groom in the message (for example, "Seth and I were delighted . . .").
- A group gift from coworkers or your parents' business associates may be acknowledged with only one note.
- A group gift from family or friends requires a thank-you sent to each individual.
- Blue or black ink are appropriate colors for wedding thank-you notes.
- Always refer to the gift itself (for example, "Your cookbook was such a thoughtful gift. We have used it several times already . . .").
- Gifts of money may be acknowledged by expressing how you used the money, or plan to use it (for example, "Your generous gift helped us to purchase the new VCR we didn't think we would be able to afford right now . . .").
- Address the recipient as you would commonly do—in other words, formally, if you do not know them well; familiarly, if you do (for example, "Dear Jim" . . . "Dear Aunt Mae" . . . "Dear Mr. and Mrs. MacGregor").
- Use familiar or formal closing forms, depending on how well you know the recipient (For example, "Love" . . . "Sincerely").
- Be prompt! The longer you put off writing your thank-you notes,

the harder it will be to do. Also, the longer you put it off, the more you will forget, the more the joy and excitement will dim, and the more you will look upon it as the completion of a chore, rather than as a sincere pleasure.

PRESERVING MEMORIES

Your wedding day never really ends, as long as you can remember and bring it back again. There are some important items—as well as memories—that should be preserved.

Wedding Gown

Have your wedding gown professionally cleaned, with special attention to lace, sequins, beads, and any possible stains. Ask around for the cleaners in your area with the best reputation for cleaning and preserving wedding gowns. It may cost a little to do it right, but it will ensure keeping it safe and preserving it for yourself and future generations.

Gowns are usually stored in a box or bag with a special blue paper that prevents them from yellowing. Store your gown in a dark, dry place. Light causes yellowing, and dampness can cause mildew.

Wedding Book

Select the album style and contents that suit you best. There are many different kinds of wedding albums, from handmade papers to three-ring binders. (A three-ring binder wedding book allows you to add your own pages, and add things you may remember later.) Include memories from your wedding, photographs, and keepsakes— such as a napkin with your names and wedding date or your slip from the temple with your sealing time. You may want to include pressed flowers from the wedding or a love note from your husband. In addition to your wedding celebration memories, include facts about and photographs of yourself and your new husband at the time of the wedding. You might want to include such information as:

- personal information, such as height, weight, hair color, eye color, and clothing sizes.
- preferences, such as favorite foods, movies, songs, books, and activities.
- interests and hobbies, such as music, theatre, animals, travel, flowers, cars, and photography.
- past experiences, such as schooling, mission, travel, awards and honors, degrees, operations, and major traumas and triumphs.
- feelings, spiritual experiences, and goals—both separately and jointly.
- dreams and plans for the future that you share.

Personal Journal

Record the last events of your girlhood or your life as a single adult, before you became a wife. This can be done bit by bit during the months of your engagement, or in the first year of marriage as thoughts and memories come to you. You might want to include:
- photographs of family members, friends, and pets.
- photographs of places which might change: your bedroom at home, in the dorm, or your old apartment; your family home; favorite places; chapels; school.
- memories of your childhood, youth, and school years.
- special traditions in your family home, and traditions you would like to establish in your new home.
- things you want to remember about your wedding day and honeymoon.

CONCLUSION

Marriage will have its ups and downs and adjustments. That is to be expected. Just remember, you have your whole life ahead of you! Enjoy it as you build and grow together with the one you love—now and for eternity.

Charts and Worksheets

WEDDING CHECKLIST

Please note that not all checklist items will apply to every situation. Use this as a reference for those things that apply to your wedding.

FOUR TO SIX MONTHS

__ Announce your engagement

__ Determine wedding date

__ Schedule temple endowment

__ Reserve temple sealing room

__ Create budget

__ Develop guest list

__ Select wedding party

__ Reserve reception site

__ Order bridal gown

__ Buy headpiece, veil, shoes, and accessories

__ Schedule fittings for bridal gown

__ Decide on wedding colors

__ Select dresses, shoes, and accessories for attendants

__ Order wedding/reception invitations

__ Hire a reception caterer

__ Reserve any rental items for reception

__ Hire photographer/videographer
__ Order flowers for attendants
__ Order flowers for reception
__ Determine reception entertainment
__ Hire musicians/DJ for reception
__ Plan reception decorations
__ Reserve location for wedding breakfast/luncheon
__ Start planning honeymoon
__ Check marriage license requirements
__ Order birth certificate and passport
   (if needed for marriage license or honeymoon)

THREE TO FOUR MONTHS

__ Address invitations
__ Purchase wedding rings and engraving
__ Plan lodging, transportation, and activities for out-of-town guests
__ Reserve wedding night accommodations
__ Plan reception program, if desired

TWO TO THREE MONTHS

__ Register for gifts
__ Order wedding cake/groom's cake
__ Reserve transportation between reception and wedding night
   accommodations
__ Purchase gifts for attendants
__ Schedule wedding portrait
__ Ask someone to sit at guest book table and receive gifts
__ Arrange for extra servers or kitchen help as needed

SIX TO EIGHT WEEKS

__ Arrange for apartment or house rental and utility deposits
__ Mail wedding invitations

__ Mail wedding breakfast/luncheon invitations, if separate

__ Reserve wedding attire for groom, male attendants, and fathers of the bridal couple

__ Determine hairstyle and makeup

__ Schedule final fitting of gown

__ Have wedding portrait taken

__ Have blood test and medical exam

__ Obtain marriage license

__ Purchase guest book and pens

__ Purchase cake knife, if needed

__ Purchase party favors

__ Plan bridesmaid luncheon

__ Schedule interview with bishop and stake president

__ Buy temple clothes and garments

__ Keep RSVP record, if requested

__ Finalize menu with reception caterer

__ Send thank-you notes as gifts are received

__ Check with local newspapers on wedding announcement policy

__ Make appointment with hairdresser

__ Make appointment with manicurist

TWO TO SIX WEEKS

__ Plan reception layout for receiving line, tables, musicians, and guest book

__ Finalize any plans for reception program

__ Print programs for reception

__ Arrange family temple night gathering

__ Arrange final fitting of bride's attendants' dresses

__ Break in shoes for wedding gown

__ Finalize wedding breakfast/luncheon plans

__ Make a detailed schedule for wedding party

__ Meet with photographer/videographer to discuss details

__ Meet with musicians to discuss details

__ Reconfirm with all service providers, including florist, bakery, rental companies, etc.

__ Confirm honeymoon reservations

__ Start packing for honeymoon

__ Continue writing thank-you notes as gifts arrive

THE WEEK BEFORE

__ Pick up all remaining wedding attire and check fit

__ Give final guest count to reception caterer

__ Provide final guest count for wedding breakfast/luncheon

__ Gather items to take to the temple

__ Gather items to take to the reception

__ Finish packing for honeymoon

__ Pick up tickets and travelers' checks for honeymoon

__ Arrange for florist or a friend to deliver flowers to temple

__ Arrange for someone to bring guest book and pens, cake knife, napkins, etc., to reception

__ Arrange for someone to transport gifts, flowers, and decorations from the reception site

__ Arrange for someone to mail announcements the day after the wedding

__ Arrange for someone to return rented items, such as tuxedos, slip, cake pillars, etc.

__ Provide each member of the wedding party, other family members, and close friends with a detailed schedule of the day's events

IMPORTANT NAMES AND NUMBERS

My parents:

His parents:

Bishop:

Stake President:

Temple:

Best Man:

Tuxedo Rental:

Bridesmaids:

Bridal Shop:

Seamstress:

Florist:

Photographer/Videographer:

Doctor:

Travel Agent:

Hair Stylist:

Beauty Services:

Reception Center:

Caterer:

Cake Decorator:

Printer–Announcements:

Jeweler:

Performers for Reception:

Hotels, Bed and Breakfasts:

OTHERS:

BUDGET WORKSHEET

Expense	Who Pays
Bride's rings	
Groom's ring	
Invitations and postage	
Engagement photographs	
Temple clothing	
Bride	
Groom	
Bride's attire	
Dress	
Alterations	
Headpiece and veil	
Slip	
Jewelry	
Shoes	
Hose	
Groom's attire	
Beauty services	
Hair	
Makeup	
Manicure	
Marriage license	
Medical costs	

Estimated Cost	Actual Cost	Deposit	Balance Due

Expense	Who Pays
Gifts	
Bride (optional)	
Groom (optional)	
Bride's attendants	
Groom's attendants	
Parents and grandparents	
Others	
Bridesmaid luncheon	
Photography	
Videography	
Flowers	
Bouquet for bride	
Bouquets for bride's attendants	
Corsages for mothers and grandmothers	
Boutonniere for groom	
Boutonnieres for fathers, grandfathers, and all male attendants	
Wedding breakfast/luncheon	
Cake	
Wedding cake	
Groom's cake	
Delivery and set-up	
Cake top and flowers	
Cake knife	

Estimated Cost	Actual Cost	Deposit	Balance Due

Expense	Who Pays
Reception	
Reception site	
Food/catering	
Tents/canopies	
Tables and chairs	
Linens and tableware	
Centerpieces	
Napkins	
Flowers	
Decorations	
Music	
Entertainment	
Reception programs	
Lighting/special effects	
Heaters/lanterns	
Guest book and pen	
Favors	
Wedding night accomodations and travel	
Honeymoon	
Accommodations	
Travel	
Food	
Entertainment	
Souvenirs	

Estimated Cost	Actual Cost	Deposit	Balance Due

Expense	Who Pays
Thank-you notes and postage	
Photo album	
Living expenses	
Rental deposit	
First rental or house payment	
Utilities deposit	
Moving or storage	
Household needs	
Food and kitchen supplies	
Other	
Miscellaneous	

Estimated Cost	Actual Cost	Deposit	Balance Due

LIST OF BRIDE'S ATTENDANTS

Name

Address

Phone/E-mail

Sizes   Gift

Name

Address

Phone/E-mail

Sizes   Gift

Name

Address

Phone/E-mail

Sizes   Gift

Name

Address

Phone/E-mail

Sizes   Gift

Name

Address

Phone/E-mail

Sizes   Gift

LIST OF GROOM'S ATTENDANTS

Name

Address

Phone/E-mail

Sizes   Gift

Name

Address

Phone/E-mail

Sizes   Gift

Name

Address

Phone/E-mail

Sizes   Gift

Name

Address

Phone/E-mail

Sizes   Gift

Name

Address

Phone/E-mail

Sizes   Gift

LIST OF GUESTS FOR
TEMPLE SEALING CEREMONY

LIST OF GUESTS FOR
BREAKFAST/LUNCHEON

MASTER GUEST LIST

Use this spread as a template for your master guest list.
Make as many blank copies as you will need.

Name(s)	Address	Announcement	Reception	Temple	Brunch

Name(s)	Address	Announcement	Reception	Temple	Brunch

INVITATION WORKSHEET

Wedding Announcements

    Quantity _____

    Cost _____

Invitations

    Quantity _____

    Cost _____

Enclosure Cards

    Quantity _____

    Cost _____

Response Cards/Envelopes

    Quantity _____

    Cost _____

Thank-you Notes

    Quantity _____

    Cost _____

RECEPTION SITE

Location: _____

Phone Number: _____

*Use this page for thoughts, ideas, and sketches on the
arrangement of reception line, tables, guest book table, etc.*

BUDGET WORKSHEET

BRIDAL ATTIRE

Item	Store or Seamstress	Address/ Phone
Dress		
Headpiece or Veil		
Slip		
Shoes		
Hose		
Jewelry		

GROOM'S ATTIRE

Item	Store	Address/ Phone

BRIDESMAIDS' ATTIRE

Attendant's Name	Store or Seamstress	Address/ Phone

GROOMSMEN'S ATTIRE

Attendant's Name	Store	Address/ Phone

Contact Person	Style/Color and Size	Date Ordered	Date Promised	Alterations Complete

Contact Person	Style/Color and Size	Fitting Date	Pick up Date	Return Date

Contact Person	Style/Color and Size	Date Ordered	Date Promised	Alterations Complete

Contact Person	Style/Color and Size	Fitting Date	Pick up Date	Return Date

FLOWERS

Basic flowers for the wedding party usually include:

	Number Ordered	Date Ordered	Pick up or Delivery
Bride's bridal bouquet			
Bride's toss bouquet			
Groom's boutonniere			
Maid or matron of honor's bouquet			
Bridesmaids' bouquets			
Best man and groom's attendants boutonnieres			
Flower girl's small basket of flowers or small bouquet			
Mothers of the bride and groom corsages			
Fathers of the bride and groom boutonnieres			
Grandmothers' corsages			
Grandfathers' boutonnieres			
Other relatives' or helpers' boutonnieres or corsages			

Typical flowers used for a reception or open house include:

	Number Ordered	Date Ordered	Pick up or Delivery
Centerpieces for tables			
Bridal display table			
Guest book table			
Top of cake or around cake			
Arches or canopies			
Flowers for decorations			
Other			

Description

Description

WEDDING CAKE

Bakery or Cook: _____

Phone Number: _____

*Use this page for thoughts, ideas, and sketches of the
wedding cake.*

BRIDAL SHOWER

Given by:

Place:

Time:

Theme or Activities:

Guest	Gift	Thank-you Note

BRIDAL SHOWER

Given by:

Place:

Time:

Theme or Activities:

Guest	Gift	Thank-you Note

BRIDAL SHOWER

Given by:

Place:

Time:

Theme or Activities:

Guest	Gift	Thank-you Note

BRIDAL SHOWER

Given by:

Place:

Time:

Theme or Activities:

Guest	Gift	Thank-you Note

NOTES

NOTES

NOTES

NOTES